PAMPHLETS ON AMERICAN WRITERS • NUMBER 36

UNIVERSITY OF MINNESOTA

Willa Cather

BY DOROTHY VAN GHENT

UNIVERSITY OF MINNESOTA PRESS • MINNEAPOLIS

Printed in the United States of America at
Jones Press, Inc., Minneapolis

3 ⊂⊃ 2

Library of Congress Catalog Card Number: 64-63341

Distributed to high schools in the United States by
McGraw-Hill Book Company, Inc.

New York   Chicago   Corte Madera, Calif.   Dallas

PUBLISHED IN GREAT BRITAIN, INDIA, AND PAKISTAN BY THE OXFORD
UNIVERSITY PRESS, LONDON, BOMBAY, AND KARACHI

WILLA CATHER

DOROTHY VAN GHENT is the author of *The English Novel: Form and Function*. She has taught at several universities: Montana, Vermont, Brandeis, and Harvard.

✄ *Willa Cather*

I⊤ is customary to speak of Willa Cather as an "elegist" of the American pioneer tradition. "Elegy" suggests celebration and lament for a lost and irrecoverable past; but the boldest and most beautiful of Willa Cather's fictions are characterized by a sense of the past not as an irrecoverable quality of events, wasted in history, but as persistent human truth repossessed — salvaged, redeemed — by virtue of memory and art.

Her art is a singular one. The prose style is suave, candid, transparent, a style shaped and sophisticated in the great European tradition; her teachers were Homer and Virgil, Tolstoi and Flaubert. But the creative vision that is peculiarly hers is deeply primitive, psychologically archaic in an exact sense. In that primitivism was her great strength, for it allowed the back door of her mind to keep open, as it were, to the rumor and movement of ancestral powers and instinctive agencies.

Closely related to this gift was her sensitivity to the land, its textures, horizons, weathers. "Whenever I crossed the Missouri River coming in to Nebraska," she said, "the very smell of the soil tore me to pieces. . . . I almost decided to settle down on a quarter section of land and let my writing go." Elizabeth Sergeant, her friend and a discerning critic of her work, wrote, "I saw that her intimacy with nature lay at the very root . . . of her power to work at all." She had been brought to Nebraska, from Virginia, when she was nine. This was in 1883, when Nebraska was still frontier territory, almost bare of human landmarks; the settlers lived in sod houses, scarcely distinguishable from the earth, or in

5

caves in the clay bluffs; roads were faint wagon trails in a sea of red grass. The removal from an old, lush, settled country to a virtual wilderness was undoubtedly the determinative event of Willa Cather's life; occurring when the child was entering puberty and most sensitive to change, the uprooting from the green valley of her grandparents' home in Virginia, and the casting out upon a limitless wild prairie, opened her sensibility to primordial images and relationships that were to be the most powerful forces in her art.

After a year of homesteading, Charles Cather moved his family into the little town of Red Cloud, where he opened an office dealing in farm loans and mortgages. They lived in a house much like that of the Kronborgs in *The Song of the Lark*, with seven children crowded in a narrow boxcar arrangement of rooms and a leaky attic where the older ones slept. Willa started going to school here; on the farm, her grandmother had begun teaching her Greek and Latin, and she continued these studies now with an old man who kept a general store down the street. Years later her friend Edith Lewis wrote of that Nebraska girlhood, which she too had known: "I remember how lost in the prairies Red Cloud seemed to me, going back to that country after a number of years; as if the hot wind that so much of the time blew over it went on and left it behind, isolated, forgotten by the rest of the world . . . And I felt again that forlornness, that terrible restlessness that comes over young people born in small towns in the middle of the continent." That aridity and drabness formed another decisive pattern in the girl's emotional nature, a traumatic one that reappears in the stories and novels as a desperate impulse of "escape" from a surrounding and voracious mediocrity. Her own resistances took the form of rebellion against conventionality; she cut her hair short like a boy's, wore boy's clothes, created scandal by setting up a laboratory for zoological experi-

6

ments, hung around listening to the conversation of the older men of the town.

Her "escape" was slow, uneven, costing years of drudgery. From 1891 to 1895, a period of crop failures and financial depression, she attended the state university at Lincoln, meeting many of her expenses by writing for the Sunday issue of the *State Journal*; at a dollar a column, by writing a tremendous number of columns she was able to scrape through. For the next decade, from her twenty-third to her thirty-third year, she worked at various jobs in Pittsburgh: for five years as a newspaperwoman, at first on the *Home Monthly*, a suffocatingly parochial "family magazine," then on the *Daily Leader*, where she read copy, edited telegraphic news, and wrote dramatic criticism; and five years as a teacher of English and Latin in the Pittsburgh high schools. In 1903 she published a book of poems, *April Twilights*, slight pieces of imitative cadence; and in 1905 her first book of stories, *The Troll Garden*, was published by S. S. McClure — who immediately offered her a post in New York on his then brilliant magazine. Her work on *McClure's Magazine* was highly successful — she rapidly became managing editor — and exhausting; probably the most valuable experience during this period was her brief friendship with the writer Sarah Orne Jewett (Miss Jewett died within the year), whose sensitive criticism seems to have reoriented her writing, away from "literary" models and toward the material and the voice which were genuinely her own. In 1912, the year of the publication of her first novel, *Alexander's Bridge*, she resigned from *McClure's*, and from that time on was able to live the quiet and dedicated life of her craft.

Miss Cather said frequently that the only part of her life which made a lasting impression on her imagination and emotion was what happened before she was twenty. No doubt the remark overcondenses and oversimplifies, but one finds an impressive truth in it when one looks at those early years in the light of her mature work. There was the deprived adolescence in the sterile little midwestern town; there were the traumatic tensions leading to "escape." She was never able to free herself from this negative theme, and under its warping tendency she was led frequently to substitute strained personal emotion and belief for creative intuition. But another, far more subtle, essentially mysterious theme was also an effect of that adolescent deprivation: this was the theme of a "self" at once more generic and more individual than the self allowed to live by the constrictions of American adulthood. It is as if the aridities of her girlhood, and the drudgery that followed, had left her with a haunting sense of a "self" that had been effaced and that tormented her for realization. She was to search for it in elusive ways all her life, and sometimes, in her greatest novels, when she left off searching for it she found it.

Connected with that search was a quest for "ancestors." One thinks of that great faceless prairie, stretching empty to the jumping-off places of the earth, where the nine-year-old child was thrust to find its identity. Where were the beginnings? Where the human continuities, the supporting and enfolding "past," the streets, the houses, the doors, the images of care and contact? Even trees were so rare, and had such a hard fight to grow, that one visited them anxiously as if they were persons. One felt instinctively, in that shoreless emptiness, a special charism in the secretive animals — snakes and badgers — that warned one to be friendly with them; one might need their help. When Willa Cather first visited the ancient cliff-dweller ruins of Arizona, in 1912, she experienced a shock of recognition as intense, troubling, and exalting as that felt by Keats when he first saw the Elgin marbles. Here, in these desolate little cities, "mountain built with peaceful citadel," were the places of the ancestors, their streets and doorways, their hanging gardens of cactus, their inner chambers, the signs of their care and contact in traces of the potter's thumb on shards of clay vessels. She was to write of them again and again, and make many pack trips back to that country. Like the theme of the lost self, this too was a theme of recovery: to recover the ancestors, to redeem them from their forgotten places, to make them speak. A great loneliness — the American loneliness — invests these themes: and something else, the need of a form of integration between the self and the human past, in order that life may be affirmed and celebrated. She was to achieve that celebratory form most fully in the two late great novels, *Death Comes for the Archbishop* and *Shadows on the Rock.*

She started late. Her first book of fiction, the seven stories collected in *The Troll Garden,* was published when she was thirty-two; *Alexander's Bridge,* her first novel, when she was thirty-nine; and *O Pioneers!,* the first of her pastoral novels, where the essential nature of her gift began to realize itself, when she was forty. But behind this late start were the years of discipline in which she had been learning how to handle what she knew, and learning what it was that she knew. A number of the stories in *The Troll Garden* are no more than finger exercises in technique and gropings for subject — in a somewhat tenuous Jamesian vein which she was soon to turn away from. But the *novella*-length tale "Paul's Case" is an accomplished piece of workmanship, showing her long discipleship to Flaubert. It is done with his scrupulosity of detail and something of his shaping, tragic poetry.

Paul is a Pittsburgh high school boy, dandyish, anathema to his teachers because they feel his contempt for them, amounting to physical aversion. He comes to their aggrieved and rancorous sitting on his expulsion from school with a "scandalous red carnation" in his buttonhole. His life with his fellow students is one of lies: he tells them about his acquaintance with soloists in visit-

ing opera companies, suppers with them, sending them flowers;
when these lies lose effect, desperately he bids his classmates good-
bye, saying he is going to travel to Naples, Venice, Egypt. Paul
has no channeled talents; he suggests no particular capabilities at
all; he is merely an amorphously longing teen-ager, "different"
from others in the exclusiveness of his devotion to glamour in
the teeth of the brutal body of fate. His existence is a continuous
fracture of spirit, between his home in a lower middle class slum
on Cordelia Street ("the cold bathroom with the grimy zinc tub,
the cracked mirror, the dripping spiggots") and the theater, where
he has an actor friend whom he visits behind the scenes, Carnegie
Hall where he ushers, and the street outside the Schenley Hotel
where he watches at night, in a debauch of envy and longing, the
goings and comings of the theatrical crowd.

One has constantly in the back of one's mind the image of
Flaubert's Emma Bovary, for Paul, too, is a creature of *les sens*,
isolated in the terrifying hebetude of his environment. And like
Emma's, his fate comes running to him with his own features,
but more eagerly and swiftly than hers; with his adolescent pre-
science, he prepares his fate like a diva. His father and the school
principal having taken away his "bone" (forbidden him entrance
to his aesthetic haunts) and put him to work as a bank messenger,
he quietly absconds with a thousand dollars to New York. There
he takes a suite at the Waldorf, buys with "endless reconsidering
and great care" a frock coat and dress clothes, visits hatters and a
shoe house, Tiffany's for silver and a new scarf pin, sends for
flowers and champagne, and in his new silk underwear and red
robe contemplates his glittering white bathroom. "The nerve-
stuff of all sensations was whirling about him like the snow flakes.
He burnt like a faggot in a tempest."

He is run down almost immediately. In the newspapers he sees
how they are closing in on him (with promises from his father

of total forgiveness), and "all the world had become Cordelia Street." Despite a poisonous champagne hangover, he does not flinch from the logic of his dilemma: he takes a cab to the ferry, and in Newark drives out of town to the Pennsylvania tracks. In his coat are some drooping red carnations, and before lying down on the track, "Paul took one of the blossoms carefully from his coat and scooped a little hole in the snow, where he covered it up."

"Paul's Case" is a brilliant adolescent analogue of the "cases" of Faust and Quixote. He has the Faustian hunger for magical experience transcending the despised soil of his animal milieu; he has Quixote's fanatic heroism in facing to the death, with his poor brave sword of pasteboard and forgery, the assaults of the swinish herd whose appetite is for violation. But most of all — because of his modern and reduced mimetic range — he has Emma Bovary's ineffably romantic sensuality, lusting like a saint for ecstasies that can be embodied only in vulgar artifice — until projected, inevitably, upon death. Within the formal sectors of Willa Cather's fiction, Paul is her earliest model of the young, artistically or merely sensitively gifted person in western America, whose inchoate aspiration is offered no imago by the environment, and no direction in which to develop except a blindly accidental one. The ironic detachment of the story gives it the purity and polish of a small classic.

Two of the shorter pieces in *The Troll Garden*, "A Wagner Matinee" and "The Sculptor's Funeral," take firm grip on the fatality of deprivation which was an inherent part of Miss Cather's native Nebraska material. "A Wagner Matinee" is a bleakly effective *récit*, holding in concentration the terrible spiritual toll taken by frontier life, especially upon women. An old aunt of the narrator, grizzled and deformed, comes to visit her nephew in New York; she had been a music teacher at the Boston Conservatory, and marriage had taken her to a Nebraska homestead

11

fifty miles from a railroad, to live at first in a dugout in a hill-side. He takes her to a concert. At the *Tannhäuser* overture, she clutches his coat sleeve. "Then it was I first realized that for her this broke a silence of thirty years; the inconceivable silence of the plains. . . . There came to me an overwhelming sense of the waste and wear we are so powerless to combat; and I saw again the tall, naked house on the prairie, black and grim as a wooden fortress; the black pond where I had learned to swim, its margin pitted with sun-dried cattle tracks; the rain gullied clay banks about the naked house, the four dwarf ash seedlings where the dishcloths were always hung to dry before the kitchen door."

"The Sculptor's Funeral" suffers from a somewhat ponderous use of the Jamesian-Balzacian reflector, but its observation of the working of the frontier curse, the habit of deprivation — horri-fyingly at home in the Protestant mentality — is ferocious. The dead master-sculptor is taken home to Kansas to be buried. There, over the corpse, the observer sees the mother, the voracious mother with "teeth that could tear," frenzied in her sterility, and all the "raw, biting ugliness" that had been the portion of the artist in youth. He understands now the real tragedy of the man's life — not dissipation, as the town-folk say, but "a blow which had fallen earlier and cut deeper . . . a shame not his, and yet so in-escapably his, to hide in his heart from his very boyhood." A drunken lawyer makes the final accusing tirade, against the town's suspicion and hatred of excellence, by which the most promising of its children have been harried to exile, degradation, or suicide. One remembers that, about a hundred years earlier, Stendhal's Julien Sorel had, in the shadow of the guillotine, made a similar accusation of his provincial fathers.

The story "The Garden Lodge" is composed on the motif of the lost instinctive self that has been compromised or frozen into a ghost by the complicated successes of American adulthood. The story's protagonist is a sophisticated woman who patronizes the arts in her suburban home. Her own childhood background had been a slummy, bohemian one, her father an indigent violinist, her mother acquiescent to his futile idealism, the unpaid bills, the mess. She has rejected all that, aiming to make her life a soberly rational and emotionally economic success. After entertaining as house guest a distinguished pianist, whose music had charmed her, she is haunted by "an imploring little girlish ghost that followed her about, wringing its hands and entreating for an hour of life." During a storm, she spends a night in the studio, fingering the piano and at last falling to sleep on the floor, disturbed in dream by that lost and violated child. "There was a moment between world and world, when neither asleep nor awake, she felt her dream grow thin, melting away from her, felt the warmth under her heart growing cold. Something seemed to slip from the clinging hold of her arms, and she groaned protestingly through her parted lips, following it a little way with fluttering hands. . . . The horror was that it had not come from without, but from within. The dream was no blind chance; it was the expression of something she had kept so close a prisoner that she had never seen it herself; it was the wail from the donjon deeps when the watch slept."

Alexander's Bridge (1912) is a distinguished first novel, but Miss Cather almost immediately repudiated it as "literary" — which had become a bad word for her — with a just recognition of what was contrived in its framework and stylish in its situation. Bartley Alexander is a famous engineer of bridges, married to a Bostonian heiress, leading in the "dead calm" of his middle age a gracious life that he loves, but nervously squirming under the constraints of his success — positions on boards of civic enterprise and committees of public welfare, the obligations of his wife's fortune. On his business trips to Europe he occasionally

seeks, or tells himself he is seeking, the affectionately gay incon-
sequence of a mistress of his student years, Hilda Burgoyne, who
has now become a distinguished actress. But he is intuitive enough
to know that it is not really Hilda whom he seeks, but a more
shadowy companion, "some one vastly dearer to him than she
had ever been — his own young self," a youth who waits for him
at the places he used to meet Hilda, links his arm in his, walks
with him. He projects this entity upon Hilda and entoils her in
its charm, which he makes her think is her own. With this acqui-
escence, the ghostly companion grows younger and more vigorous
and importunate: "He remembered how, when he was a little boy
and his father called him in the morning, he used to leap from
his bed into the full consciousness of himself. That consciousness
was Life itself. Whatever took its place, action, the power of concentrated thought, were only functions of a mechanism useful to
society; things that could be bought in the market. There was
only one thing that had an absolute value for each individual,
and it was just that original impulse, that internal heat, that
feeling of one's self in one's own breast." Even when he is most
conscious of the satisfactions of his home, his friends, the wife
whom he loves, the "thing" breaks loose out of an unknowable
darkness, "sullen and powerful," thrilling him with a sense of
quickened life and stimulating danger. He sacrifices Hilda to it,
and finally is sacrified to it himself — by the story's contrivance,
he is drowned from one of his own bridges, because of a collapse
in its faulty structure.

The finger-pointing symbolism (Alexander fell because of a
flaw in his character, like the flaw in the bridge) is trite and
specious, falsifying the troubled perception which is the story's
strength and truth. Alexander's situation is that of the woman in
"The Garden Lodge," except that the blocked, imprisoned self
approached her only in a dream, attenuated to a child's shape,

14

and she was able when she awoke to force it back into the "don-jon deeps" forever; while Alexander's demonic visitor had broken past the watches of the ego and could not be exorcised, although there was no way to establish it, licitly, within the cultural pattern that had trapped his habits.

It would be possible to sketch a kind of allegory of motives between this situation and what happened to Willa Cather when she wrote her next book, *O Pioneers!* (1913). For with *O Pioneers!* the natural forces of her gift — the unknown, unpredictable "self" — suddenly broke through her carefully trained literary habits. If there is a literary precursor, it is Thomas Hardy, but only in the sense that, like Hardy, she had found her subject in her own tribal country, in its ancient geological recalcitrance and its tragic face of blessing. Here she herself was the pioneer, of whom it might be said, as she says of Alexandra, the Swedish farm girl who is the heroine of the book: "For the first time, perhaps, since that land emerged from the waters of geologic ages, a human face was set toward it with love and yearning." But she brought to this discovery a voice that held and used its earlier disciplines, melodically and resonantly.

She scarcely knew what to do with the material, for the way it had put itself together, as a two-part pastoral, seemed to have no formal rationale, and the longer part — the story of Alexandra — had no backbone of structure at all, was as fluid and featureless as the high, oceanic grassland where Alexandra made her farm: the author could only mourn over the "foolish endeavor" she had somehow got on her hands. Ten years later, when she understood better that dark logic which Keats called "Negative Capability," she wrote of her experience with *O Pioneers!*: "When a writer begins to work with his own material, he realizes that, no matter what his literary excursions may have been, he has been working with it from the beginning — by living it. With this material he is another writer. He has less and less power of choice about the moulding of it. It seems to be there of itself, already moulded. . . . In working with this material he finds that he need have little to do with literary devices; he comes to depend more and more on something else — the thing by which our feet find the road home on a dark night, accounting of themselves for roots and stones which we had never noticed by day."

Alexandra Bergson's parents had come from Sweden to take up land in Nebraska, and their death leaves her, in her early twenties, the head of a family of three brothers. The patch of land, won by homestead rights, is the only survival relationship they have. It is the high, dry, prairie country of the Divide, between two rivers, the coarse, incalculable, primitively resistant ground of an action so ancient in character it might have taken place in neolithic times and in that other austere land between two rivers. "The record of the plow was . . . like the feeble scratches on stone left by prehistoric races, so indeterminate that they may, after all, be only the markings of glaciers, and not a record of human strivings." In winter "it is like an iron country . . . One could easily believe that in that dead landscape the germs of life and fruitfulness were extinct forever." Alexandra faces the exigence of that destiny in the almost unconscious spirit of a person driven by uranian and chthonic gods, and makes her heroic peace with them. "Her personal life, her own realization of herself, was almost a subconscious existence; like an underground river that came to the surface only here and there, at intervals months apart, and then sank again to flow on under her own fields."

She has a recurrent dream, usually on Sunday mornings when she is able to lie abed late — a dream as archaic as the whole action of her story. The subject of the dream is an authentic god straight out of the unconscious, one of those vegetation and weather gods by whose urgencies she is compelled and whose energies sustain her. "Sometimes, as she lay thus luxuriously idle, her eyes closed, she used to have an illusion of being lifted up bodily and carried lightly by some one very strong. It was a man, certainly, who carried her, but he was like no man she knew; he was much larger and stronger and swifter, and he carried her as easily as if she were a sheaf of wheat. She never saw him, but, with eyes closed, she could feel that he was yellow like the sunlight, and there was the smell of ripe cornfields about him. She could feel him approach, bend over her and lift her, and then she could feel herself being carried swiftly off across the fields. . . . As she grew older, this fancy more often came to her when she was tired than when she was fresh and strong. . . . Then, just before she went to sleep, she had the old sensation of being lifted and carried by a strong being who took from her all her bodily weariness." Like Adonis, Attis, and Thammuz, this Eros of the corn and sunlight is a life principle, extending infinitely beyond the human subject, but appearing in the beneficent image of a guardian god to the subject strong enough and obedient enough to attend it.

In a sense, that divine being is the unconscious itself, assuming the image of a strength greater than the personal. Because of the primitive authenticity of the image, it seems right to see reflected here, also, something of the instinctive process by which the book came to be written, as well as those others of Willa Cather's works whose structure obeys laws more obscure and fundamental than literary precepts or even than her own ideas of her purposes: it is the "something else — the thing by which our feet find the road home on a dark night" — a power like that which carried Alexandra in her dream, "larger and stronger and swifter" than conscious intent. The two parts of the Nebraska pastoral — Alexandra's part and that called "The White Mulberry Tree" — are wrought into one form by an instinct as sure as the cycle of sea-

17

sons, a cycle which itself seems to be the natural commanding form of the novel. The story of Alexandra engages the whole work in the rhythms of the land, powerful tidal urgencies of weather and seasons and their erosions of human life, while the episode of "The White Mulberry Tree" — the love story of Alexandra's young brother Emil and the Bohemian girl Marie Shabata — flashes across those deeper rhythms like a swift springtime, lyrical, brilliant, painful. The episode is saturated with light, bronze and gold on the wide warm fields of grain that smell like baking bread, and gold and green under the leaves of the orchard where Emil and Marie meet their sudden doom, murdered as they lie in first embrace; so that the light ripening the land seems the one great reality, and the blood of the two young lives poured dark into the earth a sacrifice to it.

The Song of the Lark (1915) is a ponderously bulky novel that suffers from autobiographic compulsion. Ostensibly it is modeled on the career of the Swedish opera singer Olive Fremstad. However, Willa Cather's friend Elizabeth Sergeant wrote that she "was deeply — by her own account — identified with her character [Thea Kronborg], who had many of her traits and had undergone many of her own experiences." The setting is changed to Moonstone, Colorado, a small town in the desert west of Denver. Thea, a gifted child in a suffocatingly crowded and brutally inept family, takes her first music lessons from a pathetic, drunken old German; for proper lessons in Chicago she is financed by a brakeman on the Denver train, who is in love with her and who is shortly killed in an accident; from Chicago she goes on to supreme success in New York, where her promoter is a wealthy young dandy, also in love with her. The end of Thea's story explores both the splendors and penalties of success, the bleak asceticism which the artist pays for the presumptions of his gift. The naturalistic, circumstantial form to which the subject lent itself carried its usual vulnerability to "thesis" writing, a weakness inherent also in Miss Cather's attraction to the subject of the artist's struggle. The result is invented plot situations, sagging proportions, made-up dialogue, and a prose that often goes lax. In her preface to a later edition, she wrote that the book should have ended before the successful phase of Thea's career: "What I cared about, and still care about, was the girl's escape; the play of blind chance, the way in which commonplace occurrences fell together to liberate her from commonness." But this too is a thesis, indicating the way in which traumatic personal memory — of her own "escape" — turned into obsessive idea.

"Life began for me," she said, "when I ceased to admire and began to remember." But there is more than one kind of remembering. There is personal memory bound up with the chronology of one's own life and with ego-tensions and resistances. There is what Proust called "bodily memory," which, because it is physical and sensory, may be at once personal and more than personal, for the impulses of the senses register common qualities of experience, timeless as sun and earth, breath and flesh. And there is what the Greeks call *anamnesis*, memory of "important" things, matters whose significance is part of one's heritage — a kind of *commemoration* since it involves other and profounder memories than one's own, buried perhaps as deep as instinct and aroused mysteriously as instinct. There is still a great deal in *The Song of the Lark* that is of the older orders of memory, more broadly based than that of the ego, more essential and more original — in that sense of the word which implies "origins." Toward the end of *O Pioneers!* when Alexandra is almost broken by young Emil's death, she goes to his grave in the night during a storm, and is found there in the morning, drenched, icy, and nearly unconscious, by Crazy Ivar, an old man who lives in a clay bank like a coyote and who can talk with animals and heal them. He and

19

Alexandra have always understood each other. She tells him: "After you once get cold clear through, the feeling of the rain on you is sweet. . . . It carries you back into the dark, before you were born; you can't see things, but they come to you, somehow, and you know them and aren't afraid of them. Maybe it's like that with the dead. If they feel anything at all, it's the old things, before they were born . . ." In *The Song of the Lark*, Thea, an adolescent only beginning to break through the ugliness and mediocrity surrounding her, hears in a symphony a voice immensely ancient and yet sounding within herself: "a soul new and yet old, that had dreamed something despairing, something glorious, in the dark before it was born; a soul obsessed by what it did not know, under the cloud of a past it could not recall."

Thea tries to hold that "soul" under her cloak, as if it were a child or another self that must be protected in tenderness and darkness lest it be snatched from her before it could grow: "There was some power abroad in the world bent upon taking away from her that feeling with which she had come out of the concert hall. Everything seemed to sweep down on her to tear it out from under her cape. If one had that, the world became one's enemy; people, buildings, wagons, cars, rushed at one to crush it under, to make one let go of it." Like Alexandra's, Thea Kronborg's nature had been formed close to the land, and toughened and simplified in that matrix. She is able to harbor the instinctive self, with its ancient gifts like those a child receives in fairy tales from dwarfs and witches constrained to bless him, because she recognizes both its transcendence and the personal disciplines needed to redeem it from "the cloud of a past it could not recall," to give it feature, to bring it to birth by her own labor.

The voice heard in the symphony is associated with the western desert of her childhood. The desert had moved mysteriously with apparitions older than history, mirages of silver lakes where one saw reflected the images of cattle magnified to a preposterous height and looking like mammoths, "prehistoric beasts standing solitary in the waters that for many thousands of years actually washed over that desert: the mirage itself may be the ghost of that long-vanished sea." Further south were the ruined dwellings of "the Ancient People." Here, in miniature cities honeycombed into clefts of the canyons, were human features of a past extending "back into the dark," a racial history speaking of immemorial experience with a voice of silence: steep trails worn deep into the rock by the Ancient People's generations carrying water up the canyon wall to their hanging gardens, signs of their mysteries, their food, their fire. "Food, fire, water, and something else — even here, in this crack in the world, so far back in the night of the past! Down here at the beginning, that painful thing was already stirring; the seed of sorrow, and of so much delight. . . . A vanished race; but along the trails, in the stream, under the spreading cactus, there still glittered in the sun the bits of their frail clay vessels, fragments of their desire." The discovery of the cliff-dwellings is for Thea Kronborg — as it was for her author — a materialized revelation of something unknown and yet remembered, something ancestral and legendary yet recognizable as an image responding from within the self, an *anamnesis* borne directly to the senses by external forms. Her own gift as a singer seems to her the same impulse that made those forms, given to her in order to salvage their meaning.

In Miss Cather's next book, *My Ántonia* (1918), there occurs a majestic, mysterious image that suggests, in another way, the timeless aspect of the subject matter which seems most naturally her own. Jim Burden (the narrator of the story) and some "hired girls" from the little Nebraska town of Black Hawk have spent a lazy afternoon by the river, ending with a picnic supper. "Presently we saw a curious thing: There were no clouds, the sun was

going down in a limpid, gold-washed sky. Just as the lower edge
of the red disk rested on the high fields against the horizon, a
great black figure suddenly appeared on the face of the sun. We
sprang to our feet, straining our eyes toward it. In a moment we
realized what it was. On some upland farm, a plough had been
left standing in the field. The sun was sinking just behind it.
Magnified across the distance by the horizontal light, it stood out
against the sun, was exactly contained within the circle of the
disk; the handles, the tongue, the share — black against the
molten red. There it was, heroic in size, a picture writing on the
sun. Even while we whispered about it, our vision disappeared;
the ball dropped and dropped until the red tip went beneath the
earth. The fields below us were dark, the sky was growing pale,
and that forgotten plough had sunk back to its own littleness
somewhere on the prairie." The image could have been carved,
as a sacred life-symbol, on the stones of a lost temple of Yucatan,
or in a tomb of the Valley of Kings. The plow itself, forgotten on
that upland farm, could have been left there by some farmer of
Chaldea.

The story is as much Jim Burden's as it is Ántonia's. The two
children share the initiatory experiences of the wild land to which
their parents have brought them. Jim's family, like Willa Cather's,
are from Virginia; Ántonia Shimerda's family are Bohemians who
have come to take up homestead rights in the new country. Jim's
family live in a house, Ántonia's in a cave in a clay bank, the
children sleeping in holes tunneled into the gumbo mud. Around
them is "nothing but land: not a country at all, but the material
out of which countries are made." It is like the sea, featureless
and barren, but running with obscure, unaccountable movement
as of the rushing of theromorphic gods: "I felt that the grass was
the country, as the water is the sea. The red of the grass made all
the great prairie the colour . . . of certain seaweeds when they

are first washed up. And there was so much motion in it; the whole country seemed, somehow, to be running . . . as if the shaggy grass were a sort of loose hide, and underneath it herds of wild buffalo were galloping, galloping . . ." The ends of the earth are very near. "The light air about me told me that the world ended here": one had only to walk straight on through the red grass to the edge of the world where there would be only sun and sky left.

Out of homely American detail are composed certain friezelike entablatures that have the character of ancient ritual and sculpture. There is the suicide and funeral of Mr. Shimerda, Ántonia's father, a gifted musician who could, finally, not bear the animal life to which the first generation of pioneers was subjected. For his suicide he dressed himself fastidiously in the fine clothes of the concert hall, went out to the cow barn, and shot himself. It was dead winter, and his corpse had got frozen to the ground before it was discovered. It was left there safely till the day of the funeral, when the hired men from the Burden farm "went ahead on horseback to cut the body loose from the pool of blood in which it was frozen fast to the ground." The Shimerdas were Roman Catholic, an anomaly in that predominantly Protestant neighborhood of farmers, and as a suicide he could not be buried in Catholic ground, so his grave was made at a crossroads in the age-old superstition clinging to the suicide. But no roads ever crossed over his grave. "The road from the north curved a little to the east just there, and the road from the west swung out a little to the south; so that the grave, with its tall red grass that was never mowed, was like a little island." And Jim Burden says, "I loved the dim superstition, the propitiatory intent, that had put the grave there; and still more I loved the spirit that could not carry out the sentence — the error from the surveyed lines, the clemency of the soft earth roads along which the home-coming wagons rattled after sunset."

There are the hired men on the farm, Jake and Otto, who, with the "sag of their tired shoulders against the whitewashed wall," form a mute memorial as dignified and tender in outline as a Greek stele — nomadic figures who bear with them the ancient pathos of mysterious coming and mysterious departure, "without warning . . . on the westbound train one morning, in their Sunday clothes, with their oilcloth valises — and I never saw them again." And there are the hired girls, girls who like Ántonia came from the farming community to take domestic work in the town of Black Hawk; robust, exuberant, and held in contempt by the townspeople, these girls appear like a sunlit band of caryatids, or like the succession of peasant girls who loved generously and suffered tragically in old ballads, or like the gay interlinked chain of girls in Proust's *A l'ombre des jeunes filles en fleurs.* "When I closed my eyes," Jim Burden says, "I could hear them all laughing — the Danish laundry girls and the three Bohemian Marys. . . . It came over me, as it had never done before, the relation between girls like those and the poetry of Virgil. If there were no girls like them in the world, there would be no poetry. I understood that clearly, for the first time."

Jim Burden, who goes away to the city and returns to the Nebraska farmland only after long intervals, is able to register that Chekhovian "suffering of change" which enters Willa Cather's work during this period. On his last return both he and Ántonia are middle-aged, Jim a weary intellectual nomad, Ántonia married to a Bohemian farmer with a brood of children about her, gay in her orchards and her kitchen. With scarcely a tooth in her head, save for some broken brown snags, she is still able to leave "images in the mind that did not fade — that grew stronger with time . . . She lent herself to immemorial human attitudes which we recognize by instinct as universal and true." The suffering of change, the sense of irreparable loss in time, is one polarity of the

work; the other polarity is the timelessness of those images associated with Ántonia, with the grave of the suicide at the crossroads, with the mute fortitude of the hired men and the pastoral
poetry of the hired girls, and most of all with the earth itself,
carrying in mysterious stroke, like the plow hieroglyphed on the
sun, signs of an original and ultimate relationship between man
and cosmos.

In 1920 Miss Cather collected a number of her earlier short
pieces under the title *Youth and the Bright Medusa;* four of
them were reprinted from *The Troll Garden,* and the others,
which had appeared in *McClure's Magazine,* have merely the
quality of competence. She spent four years writing the next
novel, *One of Ours* (1922), and it is the least attractive of her
books. One would like to see it quietly buried without remark;
but the reasons for its dreariness are instructive. The form of the
book is the naturalistic, circumstantial form of *The Song of the
Lark,* with the same temptation to "thesis," but grayer circumstances and almost insufferably relaxed style. The story is the
fictionized account of a young cousin of hers who was killed at
Cantigny in 1918. Claude Wheeler is a Nebraska farm boy, of
somewhat finer fiber than others, painfully thwarted in sensibility because of the meagerness of his education and the bleak-
ness of his small-town environment: there ought, he feels, to be
"something splendid" about life. His dull miseries are followed
until escape comes through the war; in a strange and disturbing
justification of army life and war, Claude finds in France the
aesthetic order of which he had dreamed in ignorance, and dies
heroically without disillusionment. Miss Cather received the
Pulitzer Prize for this novel, and it seemed to justify her own
feeling about the book; Elizabeth Sergeant says, "She liked this
prize and never ceased to say, in print and out of print, that
Claude was her favorite of all her heroes." And Miss Sergeant

adds astutely, "Was it because he was almost a piece of herself, left behind in Red Cloud?"

In an interview with a reporter, she gave the most wrongheaded of reasons for her feeling that *One of Ours* was an achievement: she said, "I came to know that boy better than I know myself. I have cut out all picture-making because that boy does not see pictures. It was hard to cease to do the thing that I do best, but we all have to pay a price for everything we accomplish and because I was willing to pay so much to write about this boy I felt that I had a right to do so." Her willingness to write in a dull manner because the boy's life was dull, her rationalization of the dullness as a personal sacrifice to her intimate knowledge of her subject — for the cousin who became Claude Wheeler was, after all, as she said, "her own flesh and blood" — these are embarrassing comments on the pitfalls of a temperament that would never wholly know itself; they are the negative aspect of an endowment that remained in large degree unconscious. The ethic of human fidelity runs all through her life as through her work; she never confused the importance of her writing with the importance of even the most obscure human relationships; and it is the same characteristic of fidelity that led her to the mistake of *One of Ours*: "that boy" should not die unknown, the significance of his life should not go unrecorded. But the fidelities of flesh and blood are not the fidelities of art.

A Lost Lady (1923) is a short novel constructed on an altogether different principle, that of the "novel *démeublé*" (to use her own term), the novel disburdened of the lumber of circumstantial detail and stripped to functional episodes. The book has been widely praised as a "small masterpiece." Undoubtedly it owes its appeal to the chief character, Marian Forrester, but the magical quality of that portrait is assured by a fastidious economy of narrative means. Mrs. Forrester appears largely as reflected through the sensibility of young Niel Herbert, in a series of sharply focused vignettes that catch her brilliance and also the disturbing shadow of something illicit in her nature that troubles the bright illusion in the boy's mind. She is first seen as the slender, light-footed lady who runs down from the kitchen of the big house on the hill, to bring hot, freshly baked bread to some small boys who are hunting in the Forrester woods. The charming, gratuitous gesture is typical of her relationship with life, for she has the gift of giving; and the small boys, in their mute and clumsy way, thrill with adoration, as do Captain Forrester's famous and important guests who stop over in the little town of Sweet Water, Nebraska, mainly because of the spell cast by Marian Forrester — the spell of a nameless creature-grace, a secret ardor of the senses: "she had always the power of suggesting things much lovelier than herself, as the perfume of a single flower may call up the whole sweetness of spring"; her eyes, "when they laughed for a moment into one's own, seemed to promise a wild delight that he has not found in life." Her gift is a reckless one, dependent on spendthrift opportunities, and her opportunities are circumscribed. On a winter day, one of the boys from the village, crouched behind a log in the woods, sees Mrs. Forrester and Frank Ellinger, a frequent guest from Denver, get out of their sleigh and go off among the trees, carrying fur robes; it is a long time before they return, and they have forgotten to get the pine boughs which had been their excuse for coming. Ellinger goes back to get the boughs, while Mrs. Forrester waits in the sleigh, close to the hidden boy: "When the strokes of the hatchet rang out from the ravine, he could see her eyelids flutter . . . soft shivers went through her body." When Captain Forrester is impoverished by a bank failure, and soon afterwards suffers a stroke, her opportunities are much narrower, for fewer guests stop off at the big house in Sweet Water; then he dies, and her isolation becomes frantic. One day by accident Niel Herbert catches sight of her through an open door, standing at the kitchen table in an old wrapper, rolling out dough (she is still the maker and giver of bread), and behind her, with his hands on her breasts, is Ivy Peters, an underbred and brutal young man of the town (if he were a character in a Faulkner novel, his name would have been Snopes), who has been buying up the Forrester land. In vignettes such as these, one sees the fatality of Marian Forrester's nature and the slow corrosion overtaking it. Or is it only the corruption of an image in Niel Herbert's mind? He cannot understand her when she says, "I feel such a power to live in me, Niel." And he cannot forgive her because "she preferred life on any terms."

The brilliant, ambiguous portrait to some extent conceals or outweighs a weakness in the book's conception. *A Lost Lady* has consistently been read as a study in degeneration, not only of a character but more especially of a set of values associated with the pioneer generation of Captain Forrester; and evidently Willa Cather thought of the book this way too, for she uses the reflective intelligence of Niel Herbert to appraise and condemn the loss of values. When this happens, the prose immediately becomes cliché, the thought specious, diffuse, and sentimental: "The Old West had been settled by dreamers, great-hearted adventurers who were unpractical to the point of magnificence; a courteous brotherhood, strong in attack but weak in defence, who could conquer but could not hold. Now all the vast territory they had won was to be at the mercy of men like Ivy Peters, who had never dared anything, never risked anything. They would drink up the mirage, dispel the morning freshness, root out the great brooding spirit of freedom, the generous, easy life of the great land-holders. The space, the colour, the princely carelessness of the pioneer they would destroy and cut up into profitable bits, as the match factory splinters the primeval forest." One has only to compare a passage such as this with almost any passage from the great pastorals to feel here the hollow echoes of a prose beating out a thesis and — whether the sentiment itself be true or not — sounding false. Willa Cather's art is an art of the sensuous and concrete, a high art of feeling; the spirit of the "idea" is always deadly to it. Through Niel Herbert one feels that "suffering of change" that one feels through Jim Burden in *My Antonia*, and this is truthful and real — but it is something very different from the idea of the decline of the West that comes dangerously near to spoiling the book.

In *The Professor's House* (1925) two major themes reappear and converge: the theme of the disbarred creative energy of the natural self and the theme of recovery of the "ancestors." The book is constructed like a triptych. The first panel describes Professor St. Peter's family — the complicated relationships that now, in his middle age, he realizes are wholly negative, a formidable system of checks on the power to live. The center panel, "Tom Outland's Story," is curiously dissociated in time and quality from the rest: it tells of the discovery of the cliff-dweller ruins, many years earlier, by one of St. Peter's students (later killed in the war), and of the few months of one intense summer when the boy had lived alone on the Blue Mesa in kinship with the lost Ancient People. The third panel is the professor's private adventure: he comes very near death in the crisis of rediscovery of his earlier self, and not unwillingly; for nothing much can be made of the rough and immature shape in which the forgotten self appears — there is no room for it in the busy, negative circumstances of St. Peter's maturity.

His two married daughters loathe each other, the two sons-in-law are at swords' points, his wife (who had been deeply jealous of Tom Outland's relationship with St. Peter) carries on a curiously sinister flirtation with a son-in-law. In this desiccated atmosphere of impotent emotions, glossed by handsome social clatter, the professor maintains integrity only by reticence and courtesy, often envying Euripides' withdrawal in his old age to a cave by the sea, away from women.

The family goes abroad for the summer, and the professor, left alone in the house, begins work on Tom Outland's notes and diary, to prepare them for publication. Criticism of *The Professor's House* has usually dealt with the bold intrusion of the Tom Outland material into the middle of the novel as a "technical mistake." However, it is only with this middle section that the prose rises out of sophisticated competence and begins to move with that warmth and sensuousness that are characteristic of Willa Cather's writing when it comes from the deeper sources of her feeling.

Young Tom Outland, herding cattle to make a stake for college, had been hunting for steers that had run wild in the canyons of the Blue Mesa, when he came on the cliff-dweller ruins. "I wish I could tell you what I saw there," he writes, "just *as* I saw it, on that first morning, through a veil of lightly falling snow. Far up above me, a thousand feet or so, set in a great cavern in the face of the cliff, I saw a little city of stone, asleep. It was as still as sculpture — and something like that . . . pale little houses of stone nestling close to one another, perched on top of each other, with flat roofs, narrow windows, straight walls, and in the middle of the group, a round tower. . . . A fringe of cedars grew along the edge of the cavern, like a garden. They were the only living things. Such silence and stillness and repose — immortal repose. That village sat looking down into the canyon with the calmness of eternity." It was not only the discovery of the ancient people that gave that summer its intensity in Tom Outland's life; living alone on the high mesa, he experienced the freshness of a land that seemed newly emerged from creation. "And the air, my God, what air! — Soft, tingling, gold, hot with an edge of chill on it, full of the smell of piñons — it was like breathing the sun, breathing the colour of the sky. . . . Up there alone, a close neighbour to the sun, I seemed to get the solar energy in some direct way. And at night, when I watched it drop down behind the edge of the plain below me, I used to feel that I couldn't have borne another hour of that consuming light, that I was full to the brim, and needed dark and sleep."

This sense of organic involvement in the tidal rhythms of the earth, this baptismal freshness of all origins, become related, in the professor's mind, with the creative period of his own youth. He had expected, in fantasy, Tom Outland's ghost to come back again through the garden door to visit with him, "as he had so often done in dreams." But another boy comes, "the boy the Professor had long ago left behind him in Kansas," the original, unregenerate St. Peter. He yields to this "twin," as he calls him, entire possession, as if yielding to an illicit and slightly alarming addiction; and in the arms of his obsession forgets to turn off an old and defective gas heater. He is rescued from asphyxiation by the ancient housekeeper, Augusta, coming to dust the attic where he works. The person of Augusta is beautifully considered: "Augusta was like the taste of bitter herbs; she was the bloomless side of life that he had always run away from, — yet when he had to face it, he found that it wasn't altogether repugnant. . . . She talked about death as she spoke of a hard winter or a rainy March, or any of the sadnesses of nature." She functions, in this delicate and profound psychic drama, as the "mother," older than all knowledge, bitter and at last saving; with her help, in the attic full of old dressmaker's mummies, St. Peter is able to relinquish the young "twin" whose subtle face had suddenly become that of death.

On its fine surfaces, the book confronts the dereliction of mid-

dle age with the high, poetic promise of youth, and its dramatic
concern is the psychological crisis of renunciation (Willa Cather
wrote in Robert Frost's copy that the story was about "letting go
with the heart"). True, evidently, as that reading is, there is something wrong under these surfaces. The theme of the lapsed self
remains not much beyond the point where it had stood in *Alexander's Bridge*; like Bartley Alexander, trapped in the complicated arrangements he has made for living, St. Peter is able to
recover the natural self only as a projection — first upon the youthful ghost of Tom Outland, and then upon the time-bound and un-
couth figure of his own boyhood. As with Alexander, the falsifi-
cation exacts its penalty. But if, by renunciation, the professor
escapes death, it is not exactly "life" that he returns to, but the
intricate corruption, the emotional and spiritual dearth of his
ordinary existence. And despite the youthful exaltation of discovery in "Tom Outland's Story," there is a pervading "deathi-
ness" here also: the immortal repose of the "little city of stone,
asleep . . . still as sculpture" is the repose of death.

> And, little town, thy streets for evermore
> Will silent be; and not a soul to tell
> Why thou art desolate, can e'er return.

The psychological problems suggested by the two recovery
themes are of very great subtlety and difficulty; and in Willa Cather's insistent, unsatisfied returns to them, one recognizes the "prob-
lem-solving" function that the artist's work serves for himself — the
experimental, hypothetical character of each piece of work as it
attempts another provisional answer or resolution. Though the
two themes converge in *The Professor's House* (that is, simply
by being juxtaposed, with their relationship left to inference),
they are not yet congruent; nor are they yet able to deal with
their materials as of the substance of life; the ancestors are dead,
and the self has only enough life in it to assent to its own death.

Willa Cather was fifty-two now, about the same age as the professor, and her energies seem to be concentrated more and more deliberately on these themes. It was not until *Death Comes for the Archbishop,* two years later, that the places of the ancestors became populated with the living, in the experience of a self to whom nothing was lost or outgrown, that could comprehend all its states of consciousness as things within reach of the hand.

Meanwhile she wrote *My Mortal Enemy* (1926). It is a curious little book, artistically very attractive, a "novel *démeublé*" like *A Lost Lady*; that it concerns a malicious — though magnetic — character does not altogether account for the slight feeling of puzzled dissatisfaction with which one turns from it. Myra Henshawe is Irish, and this is perhaps the salient fact about her, one which the author understands very well (her own people were Scotch-Irish). She is seen first in her worldly sumptuousness and glamour, as an adept hostess in New York of the early part of the century, warm, mobile, intense, superb in her effects — the impression is drawn with Tolstoian deftness. Behind her, subtly increasing her glamour, is the whispered story of her girlhood elopement with a young German "free-thinker," and her disinheritance by the wealthy, picturesque Irish uncle who had brought her up as an orphan. Signs of malevolence in her charm appear obliquely — the unaccountable Irish malevolence turned against those she loves. After years, Myra is seen again under reduced and somewhat seedy circumstances, living in a rundown apartment-hotel on the West Coast, old and ill, tended with devotion by her engagingly civilized husband, who has always the courtesy to be polite to the devils that run her; she still has the grace of innate magnificence, is still superb in her effects — on her dying bed, she murmurs to the loved husband watching over her, "Why must I die like this, alone with my mortal enemy?"

The malignant sentence is not the last of her stagery. The

uncle who had brought her up and disinherited her (he gave his wealth to a convent) had had a proud funeral. He did not go to the Church but the Church came to him; bishop and clergy met the coffin and "bore it up to the high altar on a river of colour and incense and organ-tone." Myra makes her own spectacular arrangements; sensing death, she gathers up her blankets in the night, takes a taxi to a bare headland on the Pacific where an old twisted cedar leans from the sea, and dies there at dawn. She had imagined that death at dawn: "That is always such a forgiving time. When that first cold, bright streak comes over the water, it's as if all our sins were pardoned; as if the sky leaned over the earth and kissed it and gave it absolution."

Aside from the essential interest of the character, the significance of the book lies in its structural movement toward the metamorphosis occurring in middle age, the invasion of ancestry into personality (a phenomenon with which Proust too was concerned — as in Swann's aging into the Jewish patriarchal type, and in Saint-Loup's increasing resemblance to the medieval Guermantes image). As Myra Henshawe ages, she is invaded more and more by the ungovernable powers of inheritance, which she identifies with her uncle. "We were very proud of each other," she says, "and if he'd lived till now, I'd go back to him and ask his pardon . . . Yes, and because as we grow old we become more and more the stuff our forbears put into us. I can feel his savagery strengthen in me. We think we are so individual and so misunderstood when we are young; but the nature our strain of blood carries is inside there, waiting, like our skeleton." Myra dies overwhelmed by the ancestors — that strange Irish agglomerate of the dark primitive with what is most magical in Christianity and with what is most censorious, turning to the revenge of those magic snakes which St. Patrick drove out of Ireland to lodge in the souls of his converts. The themes of the ancestors and the

34

instinctive self come together here in one person, in a barbaric pattern of destructiveness. But the book leaves one with the unsatisfied sense of something unseated and unreferred, something belonging to a larger context than Myra Henshawe's Irishness, something whose resolution here is perhaps too facile, a kind of ethnic cliché.

After a short prologue, *Death Comes for the Archbishop* (1927) starts in the manner of a legend's "once upon a time": "One afternoon in the autumn of 1851 a solitary horseman, followed by a pack-mule, was pushing through an arid stretch of country somewhere in central New Mexico." The conduct of the book is legendary — with that quality of the most enduring legends that endure because they represent primal human experience, the excesses and elaborative accretions rubbed off by long handling, so that what remains is the rounded core, hand-smoothed to a satiny luster; while the people in the book, the "strong people of the old deep days of life," not only have each their legends but have become their own legends. The prose has the bland, voiced quality of oral telling — not apparently an accident, for Elizabeth Sergeant records that each day, after writing, Willa Cather went alone to a stony place in the woods and read her work aloud to test its sounds and rhythms.

Most of the episodes evoke the virtue of place, textures of earth and weather that are the basis of all sense of reality, and the relationships of human generations silently handing down their wisdom of place. Hence a sacramental character invests not only the experiences of the archbishop, Jean Latour, because of his religious mission, but also the land itself and the habits of the people living there. On that journey in 1851, after traveling three days thirsty in a desert of brick-colored sand hills, the young bishop comes upon a cruciform juniper tree and kneels there to pray to the Mother for water for his animals and himself; and shortly thereafter he comes upon a place called Hidden Water, where a spring has for unknown ages fed human settlement, and recognizes here something familiar from his own anciently settled country, Auvergne: "This spot had been a refuge for humanity long before these Mexicans had come upon it. It was older than history, like those well-heads in his own country where the Roman settlers had set up the image of a river goddess, and later the Christian priests had planted a cross." Across the "life-giving stream" a boy leads a flock of goats to pasture, the angoras leaping the stream in arrows of dazzling whiteness in the sunlight; the people beat out their grain on an earthen threshing-floor and winnow it in the wind "like the Children of Israel." One is in the presence of a way of life like that suggested in the twenty-third Psalm: "He maketh me to lie down in green pastures: he leadeth me beside the still waters. He restoreth my soul."

In Nebraska, the early homesteaders had experienced the emptiness of that wild land as a curse taken into their nerves to be passed on to their children as congenital deprivation (one remembers the gaunt house and the cattle-tracked clay bluffs, the dishcloths hung out to dry and the turkeys picking up refuse about the kitchen door), a curse accommodated by the Protestant taboo on the instinctual. The evocation in this book of the more remote American "ancestors," the southwestern Indians, redresses the balance of instinct, particularly in relation to the land. Moving through the desert with Eusabio, his Navajo guide, the archbishop comes to recognize the vital relationship between land and people: "Travelling with Eusabio was like travelling with the landscape made human." As the white man's way was assertion of himself against the land, "it was the Indian's way to pass through a country without disturbing anything; to pass and leave no trace, like fish through the water, or birds through the air. It was the Indian manner to vanish into the landscape, not to stand out against it. The Hopi villages that were set upon rock mesas, were made to look like the rocks on which they sat, were imperceptible at a distance. The Navajo hogans, among the sand and willows, were made of sand and willows." Two Zuñi runners pass them, saluting by gestures of the open palm but not stopping: "They coursed over the sand with the fleetness of young antelope, their bodies disappearing and reappearing among the sand dunes, like the shadows that eagles cast in their strong, unhurried flight."

In the Nebraska of Willa Cather's generation, human landmarks were scarce and the landmarks that were raised were like the town of Red Cloud where she grew up, hesitant and ugly and traditionless, perpetuating an obstinate sterility. The pueblos where Jean Latour goes on his pilgrimages have Homeric names and associations: "Santo Domingo, breeder of horses; Isleta, whitened with gypsum; Laguna, of wide pastures; and finally, cloud-set Ácoma." The people of the pueblo of Taos appear on their houses a little before sunset, and it is as if American life were seen in a new dimension, new but very old, connected perhaps with the source-lands of civilization in the Middle East, perhaps with Arabia: there were "two large communal houses, shaped like pyramids, gold-coloured in the afternoon light, with the purple mountain lying just behind them. Gold-coloured men in white burnouses came out on the stairlike flights of roofs, and stood still as statues, apparently watching the changing light on the mountain. There was a religious silence over the place; no sound at all but the bleating of goats coming home through clouds of golden dust."

As the Ancient People of the continent are brought alive again in their pueblos — the streets of the ancestors in the heart no more desolate — the land too, and the air, tell of creation and an original relationship. At the rock of Ácoma, steep and scaled by an old path trodden over thousands of years by water-carriers, the archbishop is overtaken by sudden storm, and stops at the top of the mesa to look out over the great plain glittering with rain sheets, the distant mountains bright in sunlight, and "thought that the first Creation morning might have looked like this, when the dry land was first drawn up out of the deep." The aging bishop, tired by journeying and tempted by thoughts of his homeland in France, chooses to die in exile in New Mexico because of the light, dry, aromatic air that had become habitual to the lungs and spiritually necessary, an air that "one could breathe . . . only on the bright edges of the world, on the great grass plains or the sage-brush desert," blowing in through the windows "with the fragrance of hot sun and sage-brush and sweet clover; a wind that made one's body feel light and one's heart cry 'To-day, to-day,' like a child's."

There is no problem of the natural self here, for the self has been living all its potentialities, embodied in an individual and unique mission, in conversation with inheritance and with the heritable. Dying, the archbishop "sat in the middle of his own consciousness; none of his former states of mind were lost or out-grown. They were all within reach of his hand, and all compre-hensible." His last conscious image is one of his youth, of the *diligence* for Paris rumbling down a mountain gorge, to take him on his first step toward the new world; but this image is very different from the demons of youth that possessed Bartley Alex-ander and Professor St. Peter, insidiously negating the developed personality: the image here is that of a young traveler, setting out again in peril and devotion.

Between this book and *Shadows on the Rock* (1931), Willa Cather's father died, a death from which she suffered severe shock, and she had tended her mother through a long paralytic illness; from the personal point of view, there can be no question of the immediate emotional provenience of the central relationship in

Shadows on the Rock, that between father and child (Euclide Auclair, apothecary of Quebec, and his small daughter Cécile) — the essential image of human continuity. But the "child" had appeared frequently before, as a psychological symbol, in Willa Cather's writings — the "divine child" of myth and of dreams, making its clamor at the limen of consciousness, requiring entrance. Now the child, the initial and potential self, is the main character.

Again the story starts in the manner of a legend's "once upon a time": "One afternoon late in October of the year 1697, Euclide Auclair, the philosopher apothecary of Quebec, stood on the top of Cap Diamant gazing down the broad, empty river far beneath him." That haunted gaze down the river, where the last ships for France have disappeared before winter isolates the Rock, is a continuous minor motif in the book; for these people are in exile — as, indeed, all the people of Willa Cather's great pastorals are in exile, thrust forth on a wild new earth, cut off from the continuities of the past. But this rock of Quebec — like the desert pueblos of New Mexico — has gathered its own legends out of the raw and dangerous wilderness, and for the child Cécile these impregnate all the steep streets, "ancestors" alive in her love and will and tangible as the air she breathes. As the autumn fog drifts brown from the river, vapors changing density and color to amethyst and red lavender, "It was like walking in a dream. One could not see the people one passed, or the river, or one's own house. Not even the winter snows gave one such a feeling of being cut off from everything and living in a world of twilight and miracles. . . . On such solemn days [All Souls' Day, particularly solemn in Quebec because it is the day of the ancestors of these exiles] all the stories of the rock came to life for Cécile; the shades of the early martyrs and great missionaries drew close about her. All the miracles that had happened there . . . came out of the fog; every spire, every ledge and pinnacle, took on the splendour of legend."

But the sense of the past — of those continuities which are most saving and fruitful — is not confined to "shadows" on the rock: surrounded by wilderness and constantly called upon for responses to primitive situations, the living characters of the book move in simple, agelessly human patterns of figures in legend. Old Bishop Laval goes to the church to ring the bell for five o'clock Mass: "In winter the old man usually carried a little basin as well as his lantern. It was his custom to take the bowl of holy water from the font in the evening, carry it into his kitchen, and put it on the back of the stove, where enough warmth would linger through the night to keep it from freezing." The child Cécile does not always waken at the first bell, ringing in the coldest hour of the night, "but when she did, she felt a peculiar sense of security, as if there must be powerful protection for Kebec in such steadfastness, and the new day, which was yet darkness, was beginning as it should. The punctual bell and the stern old Bishop who rang it began an orderly procession of activities and held life together on the rock, though the winds lashed it and the billows of snow drove over it."

There is another child in the book, little Jacques, whose mother is the town prostitute, and in this doubling of the symbol, the "child" appears redemptorally and sacramentally. The old bishop has come on a winter night from the house of a sick woman; no one else is abroad in that cruel cold. He turns his lantern on the stone steps of the episcopal residence (occupied by the young, graceful, splendid, and presumptuous bishop who has replaced him), and finds there a child crouching, crying and almost frozen. He takes him home to his small poor rooms in the Seminary, makes a fire in the fireplace to heat water for a bath, and warms milk on the hearth with a little cognac. "One strange thing

Jacques could remember afterwards. He was sitting on the edge of a narrow bed, wrapped in a blanket, in the light of a blazing fire. He had just been washed in warm water; the basin was still on the floor. Beside it knelt a very large old man with big eyes and a great drooping nose and a little black cap on his head, and he was rubbing Jacques's feet and legs very softly with a towel. . . . What he remembered particularly was that this old man, after he had dried him like this, bent down and took his foot in his hand and kissed it; first the one foot, then the other." The bishop is told by his servant that the child is the son of the woman called La Grenouille, and the old man nods thoughtfully, "Ah! That, too, may have a meaning." He sits through the night with his swollen legs on a stool, covered in his cloak and sunk in meditation — he has given the child his bed. "This was not an accident, he felt. Why had he found, on the steps of that costly episcopal residence built in scorn of him and his devotion to poverty, a male child, half-clad and crying in the merciless cold? Why had this reminder of his Infant Saviour been just there, under that house which he never passed without bitterness?"

Before she died in 1947, at the age of seventy-three, Willa Cather published four more books, a book of tales, a book of essays, and two novels; and after her death another book of stories appeared and another book of essays. We are told that from 1932 on, she showed signs of deep fatigue. The prose of the two last novels shows weariness. *Lucy Gayhart* (1935) is another semi-autobiographical account of the gifted young person growing up in a little midwestern town; despite its relaxed style, it contains certain moments and insights of great sensitivity. *Sapphira and the Slave Girl* (1940) is Willa Cather's personal quest for her Virginia ancestors — she went back to her early home there to find the materials for the book — but the impulse was perhaps too self-conscious, and the novel has little interest beyond the historical.

The stories in *The Old Beauty and Others* (1948) seem only the somewhat querulous writing of old age.

But the three stories in *Obscure Destinies* (1932) are the finest short pieces she ever wrote. "Neighbour Rosicky," a story set in Nebraska, is about an old Bohemian farmer who dies of heart trouble. There is in this tale that primitive religious or magical sense of relationship with the earth that one finds in Willa Cather's great pastoral novels. Old Rosicky, sent home by the town doctor with a warning, stops by the graveyard where a light fall of snow is settling on the red grass: "It was a nice graveyard, Rosicky reflected . . . A man could lie down in the long grass and see the complete arch of the sky over him, hear the wagons go by; in summer the mowing-machine rattled right up to the wire fence. And it was so near home. Over there across the corn-stalks his own roof and windmill looked so good to him that he promised himself to mind the Doctor and take care of himself. . . . He wasn't anxious to leave [that place]. And it was a comfort to think that he would never have to go farther than the edge of his own hayfield." The drama of the story is in old Rosicky's relationship with a daughter-in-law, a young girl from town who resents the isolation of farm life and is snobbish in her shabby town-glamour. She is alone with him when he has a severe heart attack, and she holds his hand, a hand not like that of other farmers, but gypsy-like, "nimble and lively and sure, in the way that animals are. . . . It seemed to her that she had never learned so much about life from anything as from old Rosicky's hand. It brought her to herself; it communicated some direct and untranslatable message."

These stories in *Obscure Destinies* face the child with the old and ancestral, gathering up in gentle concreteness the themes of a lifetime. "Old Mrs. Harris" principally concerns a grandmother brought to the Midwest from Virginia, and used as a willing slave by her daughter Victoria. The "immemorial image" here is of the servant girl, Mandy, washing old Mrs. Harris' feet — a conversion of the image in *Shadows on the Rock*, of the old man washing the child's feet. "That had to be done in the kitchen; Victoria didn't like anybody slopping about. Mrs. Harris put an old checked shawl around her shoulders and followed Mandy. Beside the kitchen stove Mandy had a little wooden tub full of warm water. She knelt down and untied Mrs. Harris's garter strings and took off her flat cloth slippers and stockings. 'Oh, Miz' Harris, your feet an' legs is swelled turrible tonight!' 'I expect they air, Mandy. They feel like it.' 'Pore soul!' murmured Mandy. . . . The kitchen was quiet and full of shadow, with only the light from an old lantern. Neither spoke. Mrs. Harris dozed from comfort, and Mandy herself was half asleep as she performed one of the oldest rites of compassion."

In the story "Two Friends" the central image is of a child — the child Willa Cather must have been — listening to two elderly men talking in moonlight on the street of a country town. There was "a row of frail wooden buildings, due to be pulled down any day; tilted, crazy, with outside stairs going up to rickety second-storey porches that sagged in the middle. . . . These abandoned buildings, an eyesore by day, melted together into a curious pile in the moonlight, became an immaterial structure of velvet-white and glossy blackness. . . . The road, just in front of the sidewalk where I sat and played jacks, would be ankle-deep in dust, and seemed to drink up the moonlight like folds of velvet. It drank up sound, too; muffled the wagon-wheels and hoof-beats; lay soft and meek like the last residuum of material things, — the soft bottom resting-place. Nothing in the world, not snow mountains or blue seas, is so beautiful in moonlight as the soft dry summer roads in a farming country, roads where the white dust falls back from the slow wagon-wheel." The two men talking seem more than themselves because of their long shadows cast by moonlight, persons representing cosmic relationships like those calculated by Pythagoras: "When they used to sit in their old places on the sidewalk, two black figures with patches of shadow below, they seemed like two bodies held steady by some law of balance, an unconscious relation like that between the earth and the moon." When the two friends quarrel and abandon each other, it is to the young girl as if a truth had been senselessly wasted.

Willa Cather's stature as a novelist and storyteller will probably always withstand those obscurations which happen to a major writer almost with the regularity of the displacement of one generation by another; for her best work reaches into human truths immeasurably older than the historical American past from which she drew her factual materials, truths that provide the essential forms of experience and that therefore cannot become "past" truths, either obsolescent or elegiac — although they are of the primitive kind that may affront our self-ignorance and stir our resistances. For the same reason, the dense world of the five senses which she creates in her best novels and stories is one that cannot be interpreted by an abstraction (a "world-view" of some kind); her work rests on an intuitive or instinctive wisdom, conveying "a direct and untranslatable message" like old Rosicky's gypsy hand, or like the image of the black plow picture-written on the molten sun. What she did was very difficult, for she had to give up conventional literary methods, in which she was accomplished, and go blindly into herself for essential truth. Yet it was through that giving up and blindness that she was able to speak in a way that often reveals to the reader something extraordinarily valuable that seems to have been in his mind always.

⊿ Selected Bibliography

Works of Willa Cather

The Troll Garden. New York: McClure, Phillips, 1905.
Alexander's Bridge. Boston: Houghton Mifflin, 1912.
O Pioneers! Boston: Houghton Mifflin, 1913.
The Song of the Lark. Boston: Houghton Mifflin, 1915.
My Ántonia. Boston: Houghton Mifflin, 1918.
Youth and the Bright Medusa. New York: Knopf, 1920.
One of Ours. New York: Knopf, 1922.
A Lost Lady. New York: Knopf, 1923.
The Professor's House. New York: Knopf, 1925.
My Mortal Enemy. New York: Knopf, 1926.
Death Comes for the Archbishop. New York: Knopf, 1927.
Shadows on the Rock. New York: Knopf, 1931.
Obscure Destinies. New York: Knopf, 1932.
Lucy Gayhart. New York: Knopf, 1935.
Not under Forty. New York: Knopf, 1936.
Sapphira and the Slave Girl. New York: Knopf, 1940.
The Old Beauty and Others. New York: Knopf, 1948.
Willa Cather on Writing. New York: Knopf, 1949.

Current American Reprints

Alexander's Bridge. New York: Bantam. $.60.
My Ántonia. Boston: Sentry Edition (Houghton Mifflin). $1.80.
My Mortal Enemy. New York: Vintage (Random House). $.95. (Introduction by Marcus Klein.)
O Pioneers! Boston: Sentry Edition. $1.80.
The Troll Garden. New York: Signet (New American Library). $.50. (Afterword by Katherine Anne Porter.)

Critical and Biographical Studies

Bennett, Mildred R. *The World of Willa Cather*. Lincoln: University of Nebraska Press, 1961.

Brown, E. K., and Leon Edel. *Willa Cather: A Critical Biography*. New York: Knopf, 1953.

Daiches, David. *Willa Cather: A Critical Introduction*. New York: Collier, 1962.

Geismar, Maxwell. *The Last of the Provincials: The American Novel, 1915–1925*. Boston: Houghton Mifflin, 1947.

Kazin, Alfred. "Elegy and Satire: Willa Cather and Ellen Glasgow," in *On Native Grounds*. New York: Harcourt, Brace, 1942.

Lewis, Edith. *Willa Cather Living*. New York: Knopf, 1953.

Randall, John H. *The Landscape and the Looking Glass: Willa Cather's Search for Value*. Boston: Houghton Mifflin, 1960.

Sergeant, Elizabeth Shepley. *Willa Cather: A Memoir*. Philadelphia: Lippincott, 1953.

Trilling, Lionel. "Willa Cather," in *After the Genteel Tradition: American Writers since 1910* edited by Malcolm Cowley. New York: Norton, 1937.

46